The Functional Life

Rediscovering the Way of Jesus in a Broken World

M. Declan Morris

ISBN: 979-8-9996640-1-3

Contents

Introduction

There is a very specific feeling that comes when you try to force a square peg into a round hole. It is a feeling of friction. Of resistance. Of grinding. If you push hard enough, you might get the peg in there, but you will damage the peg, and you will probably break the hole.

Based on the current state of the western church and the number of people who have been hurt by "the church", I'd bet that many Christians are living their lives with that exact same square peg feeling.

They love God. They go to church. They try to be "good people". But deep down, they feel a constant, low-level friction. Their faith feels heavy. It may feel like a list of chores they are failing to complete. They may feel like they are constantly walking on eggshells, waiting for God to get angry at them for slipping up. This leads to more shame and anxiety which leads, more often than not, with hurt people hurting people.

There are other reasons for this square peg feeling though. Some people are just tired of feeling lost, alone, or like God is distant. Some are struggling to connect the way Jesus lived with the God of the Old Testament. Some are tired of people who claim to be Christians, but don't act like Jesus.

All of these people are exhausted. And if you picked up this book, I suspect you might be exhausted along with them.

I want to suggest something radical: The problem isn't that you are a "bad" Christian.

The problem is that you are looking at many things through the wrong glasses.

The Wrong Glasses?

We live in the West. Our culture is built on Greek and Roman ideas. We love courtrooms, logic, and clear categories. We look at the world through "legal glasses".

Right vs. Wrong

Legal vs. Illegal

Guilty vs. Innocent

When we read the Bible through these glasses, God looks like a cosmic police officer. The Bible looks like a rulebook. And the Christian life becomes a high-stakes tightrope walk where the goal is to not break the rules.

Jesus was Hebrew. He was Eastern. And the Eastern mind didn't care about the abstract concept of "right vs. wrong". It cared about **function vs. dysfunction.**

The Mechanic, Not the Judge

Imagine you own a car. If you pour sugar into the gas tank, the car will stop running.

Now, imagine a mechanic standing there. Does the mechanic scream at you? "You are an immoral driver! You have broken the law of the engine! I sentence you to jail!"

No. That would be absurd.

The mechanic says, "Well, that's broken. The car wasn't designed to run on sugar. If you want to get to your destination, we need to flush the tank and put in the right fuel."

This is how the Bible actually works.

In the Hebrew language the word for "Good" (*Tov*) doesn't mean moral. It means **functional**. It means "working the way it was designed to work". Here's an example: "God saw that the light was good, and he separated the light from the darkness." Genesis 1:4

Was light morally good or was it functionally good? Light doesn't have morals. It just does what it was designed to do, so it is called tov. We'll dive deeper into these ideas later.

The word for "evil" (*Ra*) doesn't mean naughty. It means **dysfunctional**. It should bring to mind chaos, brokenness, and dysfunction.

When God tells you not to lie, cheat, or steal, He isn't trying to control you. He is trying to keep your engine from breaking. He is the Architect of Reality, and He is giving you the owner's manual for being human. This should already be lightening the load and lessening the anxiety because it shows just how much the Creator loves His creation, you. He wants you to be functional.

The Invitation

This book is an invitation to take off your Western legal glasses and put on a pair of Eastern functional glasses. We aren't throwing those old glasses away, we are just getting a different viewpoint.

Imagine someone says, "Look into this window and tell me what is in the room." You look and see furniture, some knick-knacks, and maybe some art on the wall. Then they say, "Now look at the room through this window on the next side of the building." It is the same room, but now you have a much better understanding of how it is laid out. There was a whole wall you were missing. The first viewpoint wasn't wrong, it just wasn't complete. Think of these other glasses like you are getting that second viewpoint. The Bible and our exhaustion starts to make more sense.

When we put on these Eastern functional glasses something magical happens. At least it did for me and my relationship with God became so much closer and so much more beautiful.

We are going to take a break from asking, "Is this allowed?"

We are going to try asking, "Does this work?"

We're going to focus on the spirit of the law over the letter of the law.

I believe the information in this book has the power to stop the friction, the resistance, and much of the chaos. Over thirty years of trying to figure out the heart of God has brought me to write this book. I love Him and His Word. I believe God's family (us) have the power to function as we were designed and that we can experience the functionality of the Kingdom of God here and now. It is a beautiful thing that you probably have seen glimpses of at some point.

Please, don't have any anxiety about being functional. That is counterintuitive. This journey is about progression, not perfection. Jesus is the perfection, now let's make progress in being a little more like Him every day.

Quick Reference
The Functional Dictionary

To understand the Eastern Jesus, we must understand a little of His language. Here are the six key words that will help unlock the rest of this book. I hope this helps as a quick little reference guide to refresh your memory.

TOV

Standard Translation: Good

Functional Meaning: Working as designed. Life-giving. Capable of fulfilling its purpose.

Example: A sturdy chair that holds weight.

RA

Standard Translation: Evil

Functional Meaning: Dysfunctional. Broken. Chaotic. Anything that introduces death or friction into a system.

Example: A car with sugar in the gas tank.

KHATA

Standard Translation: Sin

Functional Meaning: To miss the goal. A failure of aim or trajectory.

Example: An archer missing the target.

TORAH

Standard Translation: Law

Functional Meaning: Guidance / Direction. From the root *Yarah* (to point).

Example: A signpost on a hiking trail. Someone pointing the way to a destination.

SHALOM

Standard Translation: Peace

Functional Meaning: Wholeness. Completeness. A state where nothing is missing and nothing is broken.

Example: A stone wall with no gaps.

AVODAH

Standard Translation: Work / Worship

Functional Meaning: Service. No division between sacred and secular.

Example: A gardener tending the soil.

Chapter 1
The Exhausted Believer

If you are reading this, there is a good chance you are tired.

I don't mean the satisfying kind of tired that comes after a long day of honest work, the kind where your body aches but your mind is clear. I am talking about a different kind of exhaustion, a soulful fatigue that has settled into your bones. It is a constant, low-level humming anxiety that whispers, *"You are getting it wrong."*

For years, I felt this constantly. I loved God. I believed the Gospel. I knew I was saved by grace, not by works. But that theological knowledge didn't seem to stop the psychological drain. My faith felt heavy. It felt like a second job where I was constantly on probation, waiting for the boss to call me into his office for a performance review. Sometimes I didn't feel like I was doing enough, not to save myself, but to provide enough fruit. It was worse yet when a favorite pastor was in the news having hurt someone. Unfortunately, this has happened more than a few times.

I have spoken with hundreds of Christians who feel the exact same way. They are young people paralyzed by the fear of missing God's "perfect will" for their lives. Some are women who feel a constant sense of low-grade failure because their quiet times aren't long enough or their patience isn't thick enough. Some are men who feel like hypocrites because they struggle with the same sins they struggled with ten years ago.

They believe in grace, but they live in anxiety. They believe they are forgiven, but they feel like they are failing.

Why?

If the Gospel is "good news", why does living it feel so exhausting?

I want to suggest something radical: The problem isn't your commitment. The problem isn't that you are a "bad" Christian.

The problem is that you are wearing the wrong glasses.

We live in the West. Our entire culture, including our laws, our universities, our science, and even our theology, is built on the foundation of Greek and Roman thought. Philosophers like Plato and Aristotle gave us a way of seeing the world that is incredibly powerful, but also incredibly rigid.

The Greek mind loves categories. It loves to put things in boxes while using abstract thought. It looks at the world and asks, "Is this **True** or **False**?" It looks at a person and asks, "Are they **Guilty** or **Innocent**?"

This is a great way to run a legal system or solve a math problem. But it is a terrible way to run a human soul.

When we read the Bible through these Greek glasses, our view of God is incomplete.

God becomes a Judge. He is sitting on a high bench, wearing a black robe, holding a gavel. His primary job is to evaluate your performance and render a verdict.

The Bible becomes a rulebook. It's a list of arbitrary statutes and codes you must memorize and obey to avoid being held in contempt of court.

Life becomes a courtroom. Every day is a trial. Every decision is evidence. You are constantly on the witness stand, sweaty palms and racing heart, hoping you don't say the wrong thing.

In a courtroom, the only thing that matters is the verdict. Are you guilty, or are you innocent? It is a high-stakes, binary, stress-filled environment. There is no room for growth, only judgment.

This is why even a Christian who firmly believes they are saved by grace can still be riddled with anxiety. You know the Judge has declared you "not guilty" because of Jesus, but you still feel like you're standing in the courtroom. You feel like the Judge is watching your every move, tapping his gavel impatiently, waiting for you to mess up again. You don't feel loved; you feel monitored.

This subconscious view of God as a policeman creates a faith fueled by fear and guilt. And guilt, my friends, is an incredibly inefficient fuel source. It burns hot and fast, and it leaves you stranded on the side of the road, completely burnt out.

The Mechanic, Not the Judge

But here is the good news: Jesus was Hebrew. The authors of the Old Testament, the prophets and the apostles, they all saw the world through a radically different lens.

The Hebrew mind was not abstract; it was concrete. It was earthy. It was agricultural. It was drawn from the soil, the workshop, and the family.

The Hebrew mind didn't ask the abstract question, "Is this theoretically right?" It asked the practical question, **"Does this *work*?"**

When you take off your Western legal glasses and put on Eastern functional glasses, everything changes. You get a new perspective and a more clear understanding.

Through this lens, God is not primarily a Judge sitting on a bench.

He is a **Master Craftsman** who designed and built a complex, beautiful machine.

He is a **Wise Gardener** who planted a vineyard and knows exactly what it needs to flourish.

He is a **Loving Father** teaching his children how to live in the world He made for them.

Through this lens, the Bible is not a list of arbitrary rules designed to test your obedience.

It is the **owner's manual** for being human.

It is a **map** to guide you through dangerous territory.

This is how the Bible is meant to work.

God is the Architect of Reality. He designed the human soul. He knows how we are wired. He knows that we were built for love, for connection, for generosity, and for truth.

When He says, *"Do not lie,"* He isn't being idealistic. He is acting as a Pragmatist. He knows that a society built on lies collapses. He knows that a relationship built on deceit cannot function. He is saying, *"I want you to live long and flourish in the land. Here is how you keep things running smoothly."*

The Shift: From Morality to Functionality

This paradigm shift changes everything about how we approach our faith.

Western View: God demands moral perfection.

Eastern View: God desires functional harmony. He wants the garden back and Jesus made this possible.

When you switch from the legal lens to the functional lens, the crushing weight of anxiety begins to lift.

Take the concept of **Sin**. In the legal framework, sin is breaking a rule. It's a crime. It's a black mark on your permanent record. It makes you a criminal in need of punishment.

But in the functional framework, sin is something else entirely. It is **sand in the gears**.

If you throw a handful of sand into a finely tuned gearbox, what happens? The machine doesn't become "immoral." It becomes **dysfunctional**. It starts to grind. It overheats. It breaks down. It fails to do what it was created to do.

When you see sin this way, the question changes. You stop asking the anxious question, *"Is it a sin to do X?"* Which is really asking, *"Will God be mad at me if I do this?"*

Instead, you start asking the wise question: ***"Does this work?"***

"Does holding onto this grudge against my coworker make either of our lives function better, or does it introduce chaos and tension into my workplace?"

"Does spending three hours scrolling through social media every night help my soul flourish, or does it leave me feeling empty, anxious, and disconnected?"

"Does losing control of my faculties with alcohol help me build deeper relationships, or does it introduce unpredictability and potential damage into my life?"

When you ask the question this way, the answer is usually obvious. You don't need a theology degree to know that anger, greed, jealousy, and selfishness break things. They are dysfunctional ways of living.

Learning to Play the Music

This shift doesn't just change how we see sin; it changes how we see **Growth**.

In the legal model, failure is terrifying. It's evidence against you. But in the functional model, failure is just part of the learning process.

Think about learning to play a musical instrument, like the piano. When you first sit down, you are terrible. You hit wrong notes constantly. It sounds awful.

Now, imagine your piano teacher is a Judge. Every time you hit a wrong note, he slams his gavel down and yells, "GUILTY! That was an F-sharp, not an F! You have broken the laws of music!"

How long would you keep taking lessons? You'd quit within a week. The anxiety would be unbearable.

But a good music teacher isn't a judge; they are a coach. When you hit a wrong note, they don't condemn you. They say, *"Ah, I see what you did there. Your finger slipped. Let's try that measure again, slower this time. Curve your fingers like this."*

They know that hitting wrong notes isn't a moral failing; it's just a lack of practice. You can't learn to play without unintentionally playing the wrong notes. It is the only way to learn.

The Christian life is the same way. We are learning to play the music of the Kingdom of God. Jesus is our Master Teacher, and His life is the beautiful melody we are trying to learn.

When we sin, when we act selfishly, or lose our temper, or give in to fear, we are hitting a wrong note. It sounds discordant. It ruins the harmony.

But God doesn't scream "GUILTY!" He steps in as the loving instructor. He says, *"That didn't sound right, did it? That way of living doesn't work. Let's try again. Look at how I do it. Lean into My Spirit. Let's practice patience together."*

Guilt and shame are paralyzing. They make you want to hide from the piano. But the desire to make beautiful music, the drive to become more functional, more whole, more like Jesus, is an amazing feeling. It is energizing. It is sustainable.

I do feel the need to clarify that these examples are talking about unintentional sin. If you are intentionally sinning, there are most likely some deeper issues that need to be resolved. We will dig deeper into this later.

So, if you are tired, I invite you to lay down the legal glasses. Step out of the courtroom and into the workshop. The Master Craftsman is there, and He isn't interested in judging you. He is interested in helping you build a life that actually works.

Chapter 2

The Light is Not Polite

We use the word "good" for everything. You might say, "That was a good pizza," and mean that it tasted delicious. You might say, "My dog is a good boy," and mean that he didn't chew up your favorite shoes. And you might say, "Mother Teresa was a good person," and mean something profoundly moral and selfless.

We use one small word to cover a massive range of meaning, from culinary satisfaction to saintly virtue. This linguistic sloppiness gets us into trouble when we open the Bible. When we read that God is "good", or that He wants us to do "good works", our Western minds immediately jump to the moral definition: being nice, following the rules, and staying out of trouble.

But to find the true, ancient definition of biblical goodness, we have to go back to the very first time the word was ever spoken. We have to revisit the beginning of everything.

*"And God said, 'Let there be light,' and there was light. God saw that the light was **good**."* – Genesis 1:3-4

Stop right there. Ask yourself a question: **Is light moral?**

Does a ray of sunshine pay its taxes? Does a photon help an old lady across the street? Does a lightwave decide not to steal from its neighbor?

No, of course not. Light has no conscience. It has no will. It isn't "nice" or "polite". Yet, the Creator of the universe looks at this explosion of raw energy and declares it *Tov*.

If "good" meant "morally righteous", then calling light "good" would be nonsense. So, the Hebrew word *Tov* must mean something else entirely.

In the Hebrew mind, light is *Tov* not because it follows a moral code, but because it **functions**. It does exactly what it was designed to do. It pushes back the chaotic darkness. It provides heat and energy. It makes life on earth possible. Without it, everything else would fail.

Light is "good" because it works.

The Chair Test

To understand the Eastern minded Jesus and the God of the Bible, you have to stop thinking like a Judge and start thinking like a Carpenter.

Imagine I invited you over to my workshop and said, "I've built a good chair."

You look at it. It's simple. It has four sturdy legs made of oak, a solid backrest, and a comfortable seat. You sit in it. It doesn't wobble. It holds your weight perfectly. You can lean back and relax.

In Hebrew terms, that is a *Tov* chair. It is functionally good. It fulfills the purpose of its creation.

Now, imagine I built another chair. It looks stunning. I carved intricate designs into the wood. I painted it with a high-gloss finish that shines beautifully in the light. It looks like a piece of art. But, I made the legs out of cardboard tubes painted to look like wood.

You admire its beauty, but the moment you sit on it, the cardboard crumples. The chair collapses, and you hit the floor hard.

Is that an "immoral" chair? Did the chair sin against you? No. It's just wood and cardboard. It has no moral agency.

But it is **not good** (*Lo Tov*). It is dysfunctional. It failed to do the one thing a chair is supposed to do: hold a person up. It looked good (*Form*), but it wasn't good (*Function*).

Much of Western Christianity has become obsessed with the cardboard chair. We focus on looking the part and having the right theological answers. We attend the right church services and avoid the "big sins" that everyone can see. We polish the outside and carve beautiful designs into our public persona.

But God is a practical craftsman. He isn't impressed by the paint job if the legs collapse when pressure is applied. He wants to know: *Does your life actually work?*

When the storm of a crisis hits, does your faith hold you up, or do you collapse into panic and despair?

When someone hurts you, does your "forgiveness" actually restore the relationship, or is it just a coat of paint over a heart full of bitterness?

Does your way of living bring life and order to the people around you, or does it introduce chaos and tension?

To be a "good Christian" isn't just about believing the right things. It's about becoming a sturdy chair, a functional human being who can bear the weight of glory and suffering in God's world.

The Beautiful Waste (Against Utilitarianism)

Before we move on, I need to issue a loud warning.

When Westerners hear the word "functional", our brains may immediately jump to another word: **Efficient.** We live in a culture obsessed with productivity, optimization, and getting the maximum return on investment.

We think a "functional life" means a life of maximum output. We think, *"Okay, if God wants me to be functional, I need to optimize my schedule. I need to cut out all the fluff. I need to make every single minute count for the Kingdom of God. No more wasted time!"*

We start treating ourselves like toasters. A toaster has one function: to make toast. If a toaster is sitting on the counter not making toast, it is inefficient. It is wasting space.

But you are not a toaster. You are a human being created in the image of God. And the design of a human being is much more complex than simple input/output efficiency.

If you try to live a life of pure efficiency, measuring your worth by how much you produce, how many people you help, or how many chapters of the Bible you read, you will not achieve *Tov*. You will achieve a mental and spiritual breakdown.

There is a story in the Gospels that illustrates this tension perfectly. It is the collision between the efficiency mindset and the Jesus mindset.

Jesus is at a dinner party in Bethany. Suddenly, a woman named Mary enters the room. She is carrying a jar filled with nard, a very rare, very expensive perfume. Scholars estimate this jar was worth about a year's wages for a common laborer. In today's terms, imagine someone walking in carrying a check for $50,000.

She poured it out, anointed the feet of Jesus and wiped his feet with her hair. It is a wild story.

In a matter of seconds, a year's worth of wealth is gone. It pools on the floor. The smell fills the entire house. It's shocking and extravagant.

And for at least one person in the room, it is infuriating.

Judas Iscariot, the disciple who handled the group's money, speaks up. He uses a perfect **Utilitarian Argument**.

"Why was this ointment wasted? It could have been sold for three hundred denarii and given to the poor!" (Mark 14:4-5)

Can you blame him? His logic is sound. He is looking at the world through the lens of Efficiency.

The Input: A massive amount of capital.

The Output: A even better-smelling Rabbi for a time.

The Verdict: Waste. Dysfunction. Irresponsibility. Think of the *good* (function) that money could have done! Think of the hungry mouths that could have been fed!

If Jesus were a Utilitarian, if He only cared about measurable results and maximum efficiency, He would have agreed with Judas. He would have stopped Mary and said, "Hold on, that's too much. A few drops will do. Let's be practical here."

But Jesus doesn't do that. He sharply rebukes Judas and the others who were grumbling.

*"Leave her alone," said Jesus. "Why are you bothering her? She has done a **beautiful** thing to me."* (Mark 14:6)

Jesus introduces a new category that shatters the efficiency mindset. He doesn't say, "She has done a practical thing." He says she has done a **beautiful** thing.

Jesus reminds us that in God's economy, **Beauty is a vital part of Function.**

Go back to the Garden of Eden in Genesis 2. When God planted the trees that would sustain Adam and Eve, look at the order of the description:

*"The Lord God made all kinds of trees grow out of the ground, trees that were **pleasing to the eye** and **good for food**."* (Genesis 2:9)

Did you catch that? God designed the trees to be looked at (Beauty) *before* He designed them to be eaten (Utility).

God didn't just create grey nutrient paste for us to survive on. He created fruits that turn from green to a brilliant red. He created oranges with a vibrant, textured peel and a burst of citrus scent. He made food that is an experience of beauty and delight.

If you eat an apple to get the calories but never stop to admire the blossom, you are missing half the design. You are fueling the machine, but starving the soul.

A truly "functional" human life involves a certain amount of what a utilitarian would call "waste".

Rest is not waste. Taking a Sabbath can feel incredibly inefficient. You aren't producing anything. The emails are piling up. But without it, the human machine burns out and breaks down. Rest is *Tov*.

Play is not waste. Throwing a ball with your kids, painting a picture that no one will buy, or going for a hike with no destination doesn't increase your bank account or feed the poor. But it builds joy and connection. It restores your humanity. Play is *Tov*.

Worship is not waste. Spending thirty minutes singing songs to God, or sitting in silence in His presence, doesn't solve world hunger. Judas might hate it. But it realigns your heart with the

Architect of reality. It nourishes the deepest part of who you are. Worship is *Tov*.

These things are not efficient. They cannot be put on a spread-sheet. But they allow us to live life to the fullest, to appreciate beauty, and to remain human in a machine-like world. Don't let the idol of efficiency rob you of the beautiful experience of enjoying God and His creation. That, too, is what it means to function.

Chapter 3

The DIY Disaster

Let's think a little more about the Garden of Eden. If you ask the average person on the street what happened in the Garden of Eden, they may tell you a story about a magical apple.

It's a story we've all heard: God put Adam and Eve in paradise, told them not to eat the fruit of one specific tree, and they did it anyway because a talking snake tricked them. God got angry, kicked them out, and now we all have to deal with sin and death.

It's a simple story. But if we leave it there, it feels... arbitrary. It feels like God set up an unnecessary test just to see if they would pass. It feels like He got mad over a piece of fruit.

But if we take off our Western legal glasses and put on our **functional glasses**, if we stop looking for a crime and start looking for how the machine was designed to work, the story changes completely.

The tragedy of Eden is not about fruit. It is about **authority and trust**. It is about the fundamental question of human existence: **Who gets to decide what works and what doesn't?**

Two Trees, Two Operating Systems

In the center of the Garden, God placed two very specific trees. They weren't magical; they were symbolic. They represented two different ways of operating as a human being.

1. The Tree of Life

This tree represented a state of **dependence**. It was the choice to live in constant connection with the Creator. To eat from this tree was to acknowledge: "I am a creature. I did not design myself, and I do not know how to run this world on my own. I need the Architect's wisdom to function. I will trust Him."

The Tree of Life is like plugging your toaster into the wall outlet. It is acknowledging that the power source is outside of yourself.

2. The Tree of the Knowledge of Good and Evil (*Da'at Tov v'Ra*)

This is the complicated one. What does it mean to "know good and evil"? In the Hebrew sense, "knowledge" isn't just intellectual data. It means experience, mastery, and control. And as we've learned, "good and evil" (*Tov v'Ra*) really means "Functional and Dysfunctional."

So, this tree was **The Tree of Deciding Functionality for Yourself.**

God's command wasn't a random rule. He was effectively saying: *"Look, I am the Architect of this entire reality. I designed physics, biology, and the human soul. I know how it all works. If you stay connected to Me (The Tree of Life), I will guide you. You won't have to figure it all out. But if you eat from that other tree, you are deciding that you don't need My wisdom. You are choosing to become the ultimate authority on what is good for you and what is bad for you."*

The choice wasn't between being "good" or "bad." The choice was between **trusting the Designer** or **trusting yourself.**

The Serpent's Sales Pitch

When the serpent shows up, notice his tactic. He doesn't tempt Eve with something obviously evil. He doesn't say, "Hey, want to go murder Adam and burn down the garden?" That would have been too easy to resist.

Instead, he offers them a promotion.

"You will not certainly die," the serpent said to the woman. "For God knows that when you eat from it your eyes will be opened, and you will be like God, knowing good and evil." (Genesis 3:4-5)

The serpent's lie was subtle. He suggested that God was holding out on them. He implied that God was keeping the "source code" of reality to Himself because He didn't want the competition.

He was essentially saying: *"God is lying to you. You don't need Him to tell you how to function. If you eat this fruit, you can be the boss. You can be like God. You can decide for yourself what works and what doesn't!"*

It was the ultimate appeal to pride and **autonomy**.

Adam and Eve didn't eat the fruit because they wanted to be "bad" or rebellious people. They ate it because they wanted to be in control. They wanted to be self-sufficient. They chose the **DIY (Do It Yourself) approach to reality.**

They looked at the complex, intricate machine of human life and said, *"Thanks for the manual, God, but I think we've got it from here. We can figure it out."*

The Immediate Crash

So, they ate. They declared their independence. They became the masters of their own destiny.

And what was the very first thing that happened? Did they feel a rush of godlike power? Did they suddenly understand the mysteries of the universe?

No.

"Then the eyes of both of them were opened, and they realized they were naked; so they sewed fig leaves together and made coverings for themselves. Then the man and his wife heard the sound of the Lord God as he was walking in the garden in the cool of the day, and they hid from the Lord God among the trees of the garden." (Genesis 3:7-8)

The immediate result of their "promotion" was **anxiety** and **shame**.

They realized they were naked. Before, their nakedness was just a fact. It was functional. Now, it was a source of vulnerability and shame. They felt exposed.

And then they did something profoundly dysfunctional: **They hid from the source of life.**

The God who had walked with them, who had given them everything, suddenly became a threat. They were terrified.

Why?

Because when you decide that **you** are the one who defines reality, you have to carry the weight of the world on your shoulders.

Think about it. If you are the final authority on what is "good" for your life, then every decision becomes monumental. You have to be the expert on everything. From relationships, finances, morality, the future, and everything in between. You have to constantly calculate the best path forward, knowing that if you mess up, it's all on you.

That is a crushing burden for a human being to carry. We were not designed to be omniscient. We were not built to be the gods of our own little universes.

Adam and Eve disconnected from the nuclear power plant of God's ultimate sustaining power and started running on the AA batteries of their own limited human energy. From being connected to a library of knowledge to having approximate knowledge of a few things.

And immediately, their systems started to fail. The anxiety they felt was the engine light flashing on the dashboard of their souls.

This was the first instance of true **dysfunction** (*Ra*). It wasn't just that they broke a rule; it was that they broke the fundamental connection that made human life work. They tried to operate the machine outside of the manufacturer's specifications, and the immediate result was fear, shame, and a desperate attempt to hide.

Welcome to the human condition. We have been hiding ever since. (Until Jesus anyway, but more on that good news later.)

Chapter 4
The Instruction Manual

For most modern Christians, the "law" of the Old Testament is the crazy uncle of the Bible. We know he's part of the family, but we try to keep away from him. We only see him on special occasions, and honestly, we usually don't like what he has to say.

When we do crack open books like Leviticus or Deuteronomy, it feels like walking through a minefield. Don't eat shellfish. Don't wear clothes made of two different fabrics. Do this very specific ritual with a goat.

Through our Western legal glasses, it seems like God is saying, "Here are 613 incredibly specific ways to make Me angry. Good luck trying not to mess this up." It feels arbitrary, controlling, and frankly, exhausting. If the Gospel is about grace, why is the front half of our Bible filled with so many rules?

If you have ever felt this way, it may be because you are working with a dysfunctional view of a beautiful concept.

Aiming, Not Restricting

The problem starts with the word itself. When Westerners hear the word 'law', we immediately think of legislation. We think of police officers, courtrooms, speed limits, and tax codes. We think of restrictions on our freedom enforced by the threat of punishment.

But the Hebrew word that we translate as 'law' is **Torah**. And to the ancient Hebrew mind, *Torah* didn't mean legislation. It meant something far more life-giving.

The word *Torah* comes from the root verb *Yarah*. This is a term that means "to shoot," "to point," or "to cast like rain." It describes the action of projecting something toward a goal, like an archer aiming an arrow at a target, or a teacher pointing out the right path to a student, or clouds dropping rain to nourish the soil.

Think about the difference.

A **Law** restricts you. It builds a fence around you and says, "Do not cross this line or else."

Torah guides you. It points a finger and says, "This is the way to the life you want."

If sin (*Khata*) is "missing the mark", then Torah is the archery coach standing next to you, gently adjusting your stance, pointing your bow, and helping you hit the bullseye. It isn't a threat; it is helpful instruction.

The High-Performance Owner's Manual

To help understand the Torah better, we'll go back to one of our primary metaphors: God as the Master Craftsman.

Imagine you buy a brand-new, high-performance sports car. It is a masterpiece of engineering. The dealer hands you the keys, and in the glove box, you find a thick booklet. The Owner's Manual.

You open it up, and right on the first page in bold letters, it says: **"Do not put diesel fuel in the gas tank."**

How do you interpret that command?

Do you think, *"Wow, this car manufacturer is such a tyrant! They are trying to control me! I want the freedom to put whatever liquid I want in my tank!"*

No. That would be ridiculous. You understand that the manufacturer isn't being arbitrary or mean. They designed the engine. They understand its internal combustion mechanics better than you do. They know that if you put diesel fuel in a gasoline engine, it won't run.

You are perfectly free to ignore the manual. The dealership won't send police to stop you from pumping diesel into the tank. But the manufacturer knows **The Design**. If you ignore their instructions, the car will stop working. Not because the manufacturer is angry and decided to smite your engine from afar, but because the car simply wasn't designed to metabolize that kind of fuel. The breakdown is a functional consequence of ignoring the design specifications.

The Torah is God's maintenance schedule for the human machine.

God is not a cosmic bully sitting on a cloud coming up with rules to ruin your fun. He is a Pragmatist. He is the Architect of humanity, and He wants His creation to work. He wants you to "live long in the land" and flourish. Just like a parent wants their child to have a good life.

When we look at the commandments through functional glasses, they stop looking like arbitrary tests of obedience and start looking like practical wisdom for survival.

"Do not murder." Why? Is it because God hates violence? Yes, but also functionally, it's because a society where people kill each other breaks down instantly. Trust evaporates. Cooperation becomes impossible. It is *Lo Tov* (not good). It is profoundly dysfunctional.

"Honor the Sabbath." Why? Because God needs a day off? No. Because humans are not robots. We were designed with a need for rhythm, rest, and recalibration. If you try to run the human machine 24/7 without downtime, you will burn out. Your battery will die. Sabbath isn't a religious hoop to jump through; it is required maintenance for a healthy soul.

Spirit vs. Letter

Now, we have to be honest. There are parts of the Torah that seem bizarre to us today. Laws about ritual purity, sacrificial systems, and dietary restrictions can feel totally alien.

We must remember that the manual was written for specific people in a specific environment at a specific time in history, an ancient Near Eastern agricultural and sometimes Bedouin society. Just as a manual for a 1920s Model T Ford will have instructions that don't apply to a modern F-150, some specific instructions of the Torah were for a different era of the human journey.

But while the *letter* of the law might be specific to its time, the *spirit* behind every piece of guidance from the Creator was eternal: to point people in a better direction.

The goal was always functionality, how to create a community that looks like Eden in the middle of a fallen world. The Tabernacle and Temples had many images of the garden built in for a reason.

The ultimate test of a functional machine is how well its parts interact. The same is true for humanity. The Torah spends a massive amount of time focused on social engineering, how we treat one another.

The surrounding cultures of the ancient world were often brutal, tribal, and based on the what we might call survival of the fittest. The Torah was radical because it commanded a society based on the care of the weakest.

God set His people apart as an example, but it wasn't a closed membership. God's heart has always been for the whole world to function together. Look at these examples that span almost 1,500 years of human history in the Old Testament. The consistent theme is that a functional society is judged by how it treats the outsider.

In **Leviticus**, right in the middle of all those confusing rituals, God drops this bombshell of functional love:

"When a foreigner resides among you in your land, do not mistreat them. The foreigner residing among you must be treated as your native-born. Love him as yourself, for you were foreigners in Egypt. I am the Lord your God." (Leviticus 19:33-34)

In **Exodus**, He ties their ethics to their empathy:

"You shall not oppress a foreigner; you yourselves know how it feels to be foreigners, because you were foreigners in the land of Egypt." (Exodus 23:9)

In **Deuteronomy**, He makes it clear that ignoring the vulnerable breaks the community covenant:

"Cursed is anyone who withholds justice from the foreigner, the fatherless or the widow." (Deuteronomy 27:19)

The prophets, acting as God's safety inspectors, constantly pointed back to the manual when society started to malfunction. Here is **Zechariah**:

"This is what the Lord Almighty says: 'Administer true justice; show mercy and compassion to one another. Do not oppress the widow or the fatherless, the foreigner or the poor. Do not plot evil against each other.'" (Zechariah 7:9-10)

And even in visions of the future, like in **Ezekiel**, the functional community is radically inclusive:

"You shall allot it as an inheritance for yourselves and for the sojourners who reside among you and have had children among you." (Ezekiel 47:22)

Why all this focus on the foreigner, the widow, and the orphan? Because a society that only cares for the strong and the connected is dysfunctional. It is fragile. It breeds resentment and chaos. A society that cares for its most vulnerable members is sturdy. It is built on the rock of God's own character and love for all of His children.

The Torah isn't a burden to be borne; it is a gift of grace. It is the Architect sharing His blueprints with us, saying, "I know how hard it is down there. Here is the path. Here is how you keep things running smoothly. Walk this way, and you will find life."

With all these verses about how much God wants us to treat the outsider better, I know some people who have read the Old Testament or heard it preach are yelling at the pages before them, "What about all the times God wiped out entire people groups?"

There is another way to view these occasions. The analogy isn't perfect, but it makes sense of the situations to me.

Answer this question, "Is it always wrong to cut off someone's leg?"

Usually the gut response is, "Yes, of course." But, what if the leg is gangrenous and the whole body will die if a doctor doesn't remove it? The knowledge that the doctor has makes the operation not only morally right, but it is also functionally right in that case. God knows more then us, but I do believe that

He gave all those people the choice to turn from their violence and dysfunction before the destructions were carried out based on the language used in the Old Testament retellings. God was left with no choice but to save the rest of humanity from those whose violence and dysfunction had "reached its full measure".

If people were living functionally with each other, the operations would have been unnecessary.

This is a great way to transition into looking at sin with the Eastern glasses.

Chapter 5

The Archer and Their Aim

Words have power. They carry weight. And in the vocabulary of faith, few words are heavier than the word **"Sin"**.

For most of us in the West, hearing that word feels like being handed a lead vest. It is loaded with centuries of theological baggage. It carries the crushing weight of judgment, shame, and moral failure. To call someone a "sinner" is to brand them as a dirty, bad person who has offended a holy God and deserves punishment.

It's no wonder so many of us spend our spiritual lives crouched in defensive positions, trying desperately not to get hit by that word.

But what if I told you that the word God chose to use for "sin" in the Old Testament doesn't carry that same crushing weight? What if the original language paints a picture not of a courtroom criminal, but of an archer?

Missing the Mark

To understand the Eastern minded Jesus and the Bible He read, we have to strip away our Western assumptions and go back to the source.

In the Hebrew Bible, the primary word translated as "sin" is **Khata**.

And here is the liberating truth: *Khata* doesn't mean "to be a morally filthy person". It doesn't mean "to be an enemy of God". It has a very specific, very practical meaning.

It literally means "**to miss the mark**".

This isn't theological poetry. It is a concrete term taken directly from the world of archery and slingshots. You can see it used in its literal sense in the Old Testament book of Judges. There is a story about a group of elite warriors from the tribe of Benjamin. They were famous for their accuracy.

The text says: *"Among all these soldiers there were seven hundred select troops who were left-handed, each of whom could sling a stone at a hair and not **miss** (khata)."* (Judges 20:16)

Think about that. If one of those elite warriors slung a stone and it sailed an inch to the left of the hair, what happened? He *khata*'d. He missed. He sinned. (Gasp)

Did that miss suddenly turn him into an evil person? Did his commander scream at him, call him a moral failure, and throw him in prison?

No. That would be unfair. He simply failed to hit the target. The shot didn't go where it was intended to go.

When we apply this definition to our spiritual lives, the paradigm shifts completely.

The Western View: You are a Criminal who broke a law. The remedy is punishment.

The Eastern View: You are an archer who missed the target. The remedy is coaching and practice.

If an archer keeps missing the target to the left, they don't need a judge to sentence them. They need a coach to stand beside them and say, *"I see what you're doing. Your stance is a bit off. Your arm is dropping right before you release. Let's adjust your aim, steady your arm, and focus on the follow-through. Try again."*

The Bullseye of Tov

So, if we are archers, what is the target? What is the bullseye we are aiming for?

The spirit of God's commandments is the Bullseye. They represent *Tov*. They represent functional goodness, life, harmony, and human flourishing.

The Torah, as we learned, is the instruction manual that points us toward the target. The target is a life built on love for God and love for neighbor. It was the life that Jesus modeled for us.

When you tell the truth even when it costs you, you hit the bullseye.

When you help someone who can't pay you back, you hit the bullseye.

When you choose patience over anger, you hit the bullseye.

Conversely, when we act dysfunctionally, when we do *Ra*, we are missing the mark.

When you cheat on your taxes or your spouse, you are missing the target.

When you lie to protect your reputation, you are missing the target.

When you ignore the poor or mistreat the vulnerable, you are missing the target.

In those moments, you aren't just breaking an abstract rule. You are shooting your arrow into the dirt, wasting your potential, or worse, you are shooting it into someone else.

This brings up a crucial point. Just because sin is 'missing the mark' doesn't mean it isn't serious. Also, intentionally missing the target is still khata, but indicates a deeper problem. If you are missing on accident, you can practice and get better. If you are missing on purpose, there is probably a deeper issue and you need to talk to God about that before you can get back behind the bow and start aiming properly.

Sin is not safe.

If you are at an archery range and you fire an arrow wildly off-target, you don't just shrug and say, "Oops." That stray arrow has to land somewhere. It could hit a wall. It could break a window. It could hit a person.

God is against sin not because His feelings get hurt when we disobey. **God dislikes sin because stray arrows can kill people (or relationships to be less dramatic).**

When you "miss the mark" by committing adultery, you shatter the heart of your spouse and destabilize your family. When you "miss the mark" by acting out of greed, you exploit others and damage community. When you "miss the mark" by harboring bitterness, you poison your own soul.

Sin is the introduction of chaos and destruction into God's beautiful, functional world. It causes real damage to real people. God, as a loving Father and responsible Architect, cannot be indifferent to that damage. He can forgive the offense, but the dysfunction still has to be dealt with in whatever ways are appropriate.

The Physician and the Coach

This functional understanding of sin perfectly aligns with how Jesus saw His own mission. He didn't come walking into town like a sheriff looking to lock people up. He came like a field medic looking for the wounded.

When the religious leaders criticized Him for eating with "tax collectors and sinners", people notorious for missing the mark, Jesus gave a simple, profound defense:

"It is not the healthy who need a doctor, but the sick. I have not come to call the righteous, but sinners." (Mark 2:17)

Jesus didn't look at sinners and see criminals who needed condemning. He saw people with terrible aim who were hurting themselves and everyone around them. They were sick with dysfunction. They needed a Physician to heal their wounds and a Coach to correct their stance.

This should change how we understand **repentance**.

In the Western view, repentance is often seen as an emotional breakdown. It involves groveling, crying, and feeling a sufficient amount of self-loathing to prove you are truly sorry.

But in the functional view, repentance isn't an emotion; it's an action. It is **recalibration**.

It is the act of an archer stopping after a bad shot, looking at where the arrow landed, acknowledging the miss without excuse, and then deliberately adjusting their stance to align with the Architect's instructions for the next shot. It's turning from the direction of the miss and facing the direction of the bullseye.

The End of Shame

This brings us back to the exhaustion we talked about in Chapter 1. So many Christians live under a low-level cloud of shame and guilt because they know they still miss the mark every day.

But ask yourself: **Does an archer's shame and guilt improve their aim?**

Imagine an archer who misses the bullseye. He immediately throws down his bow, collapses to the ground, and starts beating himself up. *"I'm such an idiot! I'm the worst archer in the world! I don't deserve to even hold a bow!"*

Is that person going to shoot better next time? No. They are too distracted by their own self-loathing to focus on the mechanics of the shot. Their hands will be shaking with anxiety.

Guilt and shame are meant to be brief signals. They are the "thwack" of the arrow hitting the wood frame instead of the target center. They are quick reminders that something went wrong, motivators for more practice and better focus.

The archer shouldn't live in a constant state of shame and guilt. They should note the miss, learn from it, and reset for the next shot.

Living in perpetual shame is dysfunctional. It paralyzes you and keeps you from getting back on the training field.

We can let go of shame because we have a Coach who handles our misses with astonishing grace. When we ask God to forgive our missed shots, He doesn't just begrudgingly wipe the scoreboard clean. He does something radical.

Look at how the Bible describes God's way of dealing with our past misses:

"For I will forgive their wickedness and will remember their sins no more." (Jeremiah 31:34 & Hebrews 8:12)

"I, even I, am he who blots out your transgressions for my own sake, and I will not remember your sins." (Isaiah 43:25)

"He will again have compassion on us; he will tread our iniquities underfoot. You will cast all our sins into the depths of the sea." (Micah 7:19)

Does that sound like a judge who can't wait to yell at us and throw the book at us for missing the target He set up? Or does it sound like a loving Father and a patient Coach, desperate to teach His children the right way to live?

Throughout the Bible, we see examples of God as the Good Shepherd. When a sheep "misses the target path" and wanders off into danger, the shepherd doesn't stand on the hill and scream at it. He doesn't abandon it because it is "bad". He goes after it. He calls it back. He even carries it home on his shoulders if needed.

You are going to miss the mark today. You will probably miss it tomorrow, too. The goal isn't to never miss again. The goal is to stay on the field, listen to the Coach, get rid of the heavy baggage of shame, and keep practicing. We can all become a little more like Jesus every day with practice.

Satan, the accuser, wants to constantly remind you of all the times you missed. God, who loves you more than you can comprehend, wants to encourage you and call you back to Him and His directions.

Remember this fact and listen to the right voice.

Chapter 6

The Trash Collector

We have talked about sin as "missing the mark", a failure of aim rather than a moral crime. This is a liberating concept because it moves us from a place of paralyzing shame to a place of practical recalibration.

But if we stop there, we miss something crucial. We miss the damage.

The problem with missing the mark is that the effect of the arrow doesn't just vanish into thin air. If an archer fires a stray arrow and it hits a bystander in the leg, the archer can feel terrible guilt. He can apologize profusely. He can promise to practice more.

But none of that changes the fact that there is a person standing there with an arrow in their leg. The wound is real. The pain is real. The damage has been done.

The same is true in our spiritual and relational lives.

If you lie to your spouse to cover up a mistake, you can apologize and be forgiven. But the trust that was broken doesn't magically reappear. The relationship has been damaged.

If a business owner cheats their employees to increase profits, they can repent. But the financial hardship and resentment caused to those families are still very real.

Every time we *khata*, every time we miss the bullseye of love and truth, we don't just fail; we create a consequence. We introduce a toxin into the ecosystem of our world. We dump a little bit more dysfunctional waste into the environment. A little more sand in the gears.

The Law of Conservation of Dysfunction

In physics, there is the Law of Conservation of Matter: matter is neither created nor destroyed; it only changes form. You can burn a log, but it doesn't disappear. It turns into ash, smoke, and heat.

There seems to be a similar law in the spiritual realm: **The Law of Conservation of Dysfunction.**

When *Ra* (evil/dysfunction) enters the world, it doesn't just evaporate when we say "sorry". The energy of that dysfunction has to go somewhere. The trash has to be dealt with.

For most of human history, we have handled this "trash" in one very predictable way: we throw it at someone else.

This is the mechanism behind the Cycle of Vengeance. It is a game of hot potato with pain and trauma.

Your boss yells at you at work (dumping his dysfunction onto you). You absorb that pain.

You come home and feel irritable, so you snap at your spouse over something small (dumping the dysfunction onto them).

Your spouse absorbs that pain and later yells at the kids.

The kids absorb that pain and kick the dog. (They better not.)

The saying is profound and true: **Hurt people, hurt people.** Unless the cycle is interrupted, pain will just keep being passed down the line, from person to person, generation to generation, creating an ever-growing landfill of relational toxicity.

If we want restoration, if we want a world that actually functions again, we don't just need better aim. We need a cleanup crew.

The Scapegoat

The ancients may have understood this better than we do. They knew that guilt and dysfunction accumulate in a community like toxic waste, and if it isn't dealt with regularly, it will poison everything.

In the Old Testament, God provided a vivid, visceral ritual to teach Israel this lesson. It was called Yom Kippur, the Day of Atonement.

Central to this day was a ritual involving two goats. One was sacrificed as a sin offering. But the second goat, the **Scapegoat**, had a different role. The High Priest would lay his hands on the head of the live goat and confess over it all the wickedness and rebellion of the Israelites. Symbolically, the dysfunction of the entire nation was transferred onto this animal.

Then, the goat was led away into the wilderness, carrying the sins of the people with it, never to return.

What was the point of this bizarre ritual? Did God need a goat to be sent into the desert to feel better about Israel? Of course not. The day wasn't for God; it was for the people. God doesn't have psychological needs, but we do. He knows how our brains work. He knows we carry the heavy burden of our accumulated failures.

The ritual was a powerful visual aid. It taught a simple, undeniable lesson: **The trash has to go somewhere.** You cannot just ignore the accumulated dysfunction of your community. It has to be collected and removed, or you cannot have a fresh start. Restoration requires cleanup.

But "the blood of bulls and goats could never truly take away sin" (Hebrews 10:4). They were just symbols, placeholders pointing to a future reality. They could deal with the feelings of guilt for a time, but they couldn't stop the source of the pollution. They couldn't break the cycle of vengeance.

For that, we needed a better Scapegoat.

The Cosmic Sponge

Enter Jesus.

When we look at the cross through functional glasses, we don't see a God who is so angry that He needs to beat up His Son so He can calm down. That is a pagan view of sacrifice, not a biblical one.

Instead, we see the Architect entering His own broken creation to perform the ultimate cleanup operation. Jesus is the ultimate scapegoat.

When Jesus went to the cross, He didn't just die a physical death. He stepped directly into the rushing river of human dysfunction, the entire chain reaction of *Ra* that had been building up for millennia.

Think about the events leading to His death. He was hit with every form of human trash imaginable.

He was betrayed by a close friend (Judas).

He was abandoned by His disciples in His moment of greatest need.

He was subjected to a mock trial, framed by religious leaders, and sentenced by a cowardly politician (Pilate).

He was mocked, spit on, beaten, and tortured by soldiers.

At any moment, Jesus could have participated in the cycle. He had the power. He could have called down legions of angels to wipe out His tormentors. He could have reviled them back. He could have dumped His pain right back onto the world three times over.

But He didn't.

As the prophet Isaiah wrote centuries before: *"He was oppressed and afflicted, yet he did not open his mouth; he was led like a lamb to the slaughter..."* (Isaiah 53:7).

Jesus did something radical. He broke the chain.

When He was reviled, He didn't revile in return.

When He suffered, He didn't threaten violence in return.

When they nailed Him to the cross, His response wasn't vengeance; it was intercession: *"Father, forgive them, for they do not know what they are doing."* (Luke 23:34)

On the cross, Jesus acted as a **cosmic sponge**. He absorbed the dysfunction, the violence, the hatred, and the sin of the world into His own being. He took the toxic waste of human history and drew it into Himself. He let the cycle of vengeance terminate on His own body.

He let the arrow hit Him, so it wouldn't hit us.

When He cried out, *"It is finished,"* He wasn't just saying His life was over. He was saying, *"The cleanup is complete. The debt has been paid. The toxin has been absorbed."*

The Cost of Restoration

This is what true forgiveness always is. It is not just saying words. **Forgiveness is the act of absorbing the cost of the repair rather than making the person who broke it pay.**

If you borrow my car and wreck it, I have two choices.

I can make you pay for the repairs. That is justice. The debt is settled, but our relationship might be strained if they were already struggling financially.

I can forgive you. I can say, "Don't worry about it." But the car is still wrecked. Someone has to pay to fix it. If I forgive you, *I* am choosing to absorb that cost myself.

Jesus absorbed the infinite cost of human dysfunction so that the system could be rebooted. He took the accumulated *Ra* of the world and buried it in His grave, so that we could have a fresh start.

He didn't just fulfill the legal requirements of the law and the prophets; He fulfilled their deepest functional intent. He showed us that the only way to stop the cycle of pain is for someone strong enough and loving enough to absorb it without passing it on.

He taught us, and demonstrated, a better way to live. A way where pain is met with grace, where vengeance is replaced by forgiveness, and where the trash of our lives is carried away by the One who is mighty to save.

Chapter 7

The Power Source

Let's fast-forward. Imagine it's tomorrow morning. You've finished reading this book. You understand the concepts. You've traded your legal glasses for functional ones. You get it: sin is missing the mark, the Bible is an instruction manual, and Jesus has absorbed the cost of your dysfunction. You know you are forgiven. You know you are loved.

You have the blueprint for a functional life right in front of you.

But then your alarm goes off. You didn't sleep well. The coffee maker is broken. Your kids are screaming over a toy. You look at your phone and see an email from that coworker who always undermines you.

And suddenly, all that theological knowledge feels about as useful as a chocolate teapot.

You know *what* to do, be patient, be kind, be generous. But you have absolutely zero energy to do it. You are running on 1% battery, and the day hasn't even started.

This is the crisis point for most Christians. We have the information, but we lack the power. We know the manual, but the machine won't start.

If this is where you are, then we need to talk about the Holy Spirit.

The Ghost in the Machine

For many modern Christians, the Holy Spirit is the most confusing member of the Trinity. We know God the Father, He's the Creator. We know Jesus the Son, He's the Savior who walked the earth. But the Holy Spirit? He feels vague. Spooky, even. We picture a mystical vapor, or worse, a friendly ghost that haunts us, whispering things in our ear. We believe in Him doctrinally, but functionally, we have no idea what He does.

To understand the Spirit's role in a functional life, we have to go back to the Hebrew. The word used in the Old Testament for "Spirit" is **Ruach.**

It is a dynamic, powerful, earthy word that carries three distinct meanings simultaneously:

Wind: The invisible, powerful force that moves things in the physical world.

Breath: The vital, animating force that turns a lump of clay into a living human being (Genesis 2:7).

Spirit: The personal presence of God. Jesus calls the Holy Spirit "the Helper" in John 14:26.

When you combine these, you realize that the Holy Spirit is not a passive ghost. He is the **animating energy of God**. He is the Breath that powers the human machine. He is the Wind that fills the sails of creation.

Without the *Ruach*, Adam was just a perfectly sculpted statue of mud. He had the form of a human, but no function. He couldn't move, think, or love until God breathed the *Ruach* into his nostrils.

Many of us are living like that mud statue. We have the form of Christianity, we go to church and we know the rules, but we lack the animating power to actually live it out. We are trying to be functional humans without the power source.

The Rowboat vs. The Sailboat

How do you try to live the Christian life on a daily basis? For most of my life, I operated like I was in a **rowboat**.

The Christian life was a long journey across a choppy sea to the shores of holiness. God gave me the boat and the map, but it was up to me to get there.

So, I grabbed the oars of **Willpower**.

"I will not get angry today!" I'd grit my teeth and row.

"I will be kinder to my spouse!" Pull harder.

"I will control what I put into my body!" Row until my muscles burn.

This approach works for a little while. You can make some progress on smooth water. But it is incredibly exhausting. And the moment the wind picks up, when you're tired, or stressed, or provoked, your strength fails. You stop rowing, and the current drags you right back to where you started.

Living the Christian life on willpower alone is a guaranteed recipe for burnout, hypocrisy, and despair. You cannot white-knuckle your way into being like Jesus. You don't have the horsepower.

The Eastern Jesus invites us into a completely different way of traveling. He invites us to trade our rowboat for a **sailboat**.

In a sailboat, your relationship to power changes completely.

Does a sailor generate the power to move the boat? No. The sailor is powerless to move thousands of pounds of wood and canvas across the ocean.

Who moves the boat? The Wind (*Ruach*). The Wind is an inexhaustible, invisible source of power that is completely outside the sailor's control.

So, does the sailor do nothing? Is he just passive? No. He has a crucial, active role. His job is to **hoist the sail and steer the rudder.** His job is to position the boat so it can catch the power that is already blowing.

In the functional Christian life:

The Wind = The Holy Spirit. The power to change, to love, and to be patient more perfectly is not inside you; it is outside you, but available to you.

The Sail = Your Surrender and Attention. Your job is to open your life to the Spirit daily. It is the act of saying, *"God, I can't do this today. I am angry and tired. I need Your power. I am hoisting my sail. Fill me. My trust is in You."*

When you stop rowing and start sailing, the pressure lifts. You realize that your progress doesn't depend on the strength of your arms, but on the strength of the Wind.

Organic Fruit, Not Factory Products

When you live like a sailboat, catching the *Ruach* on a daily basis, something amazing happens. You start to change, but it doesn't feel like hard work. It feels natural.

Paul describes this in Galatians 5. He contrasts the "works of the flesh" (what happens when you row your own boat) with the **"Fruit of the Spirit".**

"But the fruit of the Spirit is love, joy, peace, patience, kindness, goodness, faithfulness, gentleness and self-control." (Galatians 5:22-23)

Notice the metaphor. He doesn't call them the "products of the Spirit". A product is something manufactured in a factory through loud, grinding, mechanical effort.

He calls them **Fruit.**

Think about an apple tree. Does an apple tree grunt and strain and sweat to produce an apple? Does it wake up in the morning and say, *"Okay, today is the day! I am going to squeeze out a Red Delicious if it kills me!"*?

No. That would be comical though.

An apple tree produces apples naturally, effortlessly, simply because of **what it is** and **what it is connected to.** As long as the branch remains connected to the trunk, drawing nutrients from the root system, apples are the inevitable byproduct.

When you stay connected to Jesus through the Spirit, when you keep your sail hoisted, you don't have to strain to be loving. Love just starts growing in your life. You don't have to white-knuckle patience. You find yourself remaining calm in situations that used to make you explode.

It's not magic. It's biology. It's functional. It's what happens when a human being is finally plugged back into the power source they were designed for.

So, tomorrow morning, when you wake up on 1% battery, don't grab the oars. Don't try to be a better Christian on your own power. Just sit there, open your hands, hoist your sail, and ask for the Wind. You were never meant to power this machine yourself.

Chapter 8
The Solo Christian Myth

There is a phrase that has become the unofficial slogan of modern evangelicalism. You have probably heard it, said it, or seen it on a bumper sticker:

"Christianity isn't a religion; it's a personal relationship with Jesus."

It sounds wonderful, doesn't it? It sounds intimate, authentic, and freeing. It's meant to distinguish a vibrant faith from cold, dead ritual. And in one sense, it is deeply true. The call of Jesus is a call to know Him, not just to know facts about Him.

But words are tricky things. They change their shape depending on the culture that uses them.

When we here in the modern West hear the word "personal", our brains may immediately translate it into another word: **"Private."**

We live in the most individualistic culture in human history. We have personal trainers, personal shoppers, personal assistants, and personal pan pizzas. "Personal" means it belongs to me. It is customized for my preferences. It is none of your business.

So, when we hear about a "personal relationship with Jesus", we interpret it through that lens of radical individualism. My faith is between me and God. I have my quiet time, my worship playlist, my own interpretation of the Bible. I don't need organized religion. I don't need the messy drama of other people. It's just Jesus and me, coffee and my Bible, on a quiet mountaintop.

It sounds peaceful. It sounds spiritual. It may be nice every once in a while. But I need to tell you something that may be difficult to accept:

In the Eastern mindset of the Bible, a "solo Christian" is functionally impossible.

It is like saying, "I am a personal football player. I don't belong to a team." You can wear the jersey, you can train in your backyard, you can know all the rules. But you cannot *play the game* of football alone. The game requires a team.

The same is true for the Jesus Way. You cannot function as a Christian in isolation.

The Severed Hand

To understand why, we have to go back to an often used metaphor in the Bible for the church: the human body.

When the Apostle Paul wanted to explain what the Church is, he didn't compare it to a club, a business, or a political party. He compared it to a biological organism. He called it **The Body of Christ**.

"The eye cannot say to the hand, 'I don't need you!' And the head cannot say to the feet, 'I don't need you!' ... Now you are the body of Christ, and each one of you is a part of it." (1 Corinthians 12:21,27)

Paul isn't just using poetic language here. He is making a profound functional point.

Imagine a human hand. It is an architectural marvel, 27 bones, intricate muscles, tendons, and nerves all working together to grip, feel, and create. It is a masterpiece of design.

Now, imagine that hand is severed from the arm and is lying on a table.

Is that hand *Tov*?

It still looks like a hand. It has all the right parts. But is it functional? No. It is profoundly *Lo Tov*. It is dysfunctional. In fact, it is dead.

Why? Because a hand is only designed to function when it is connected to the rest of the body. It needs the blood supply from the heart. It needs nerve signals from the brain. It needs the arm to move it into position.

Connection is the prerequisite for function.

The moment the hand is severed from the community of the body, it begins to wither and die. It doesn't matter how "personal" its relationship is with the head; if the connection is severed, the function ceases.

This is the danger of the "solo Christian" myth. We think we can disconnect from the messy, frustrating, imperfect community of the Church and still be a functional follower of Jesus. We think we can be a healthy hand lying on a table.

But the spiritual reality is that when you disconnect from the Body, you cut yourself off from the flow of life. You lose the context where your gifts are meant to operate. You lose the support system designed to keep you alive. Spiritual atrophy is inevitable.

The "One Another" Imperative

If you need proof that Christianity is a group project, just open your New Testament and do a search for the phrase **"one another"**. It appears over 50 times in the letters to the early church.

Love one another. (John 13:34)

Forgive one another. (Colossians 3:13)

Bear one another's burdens. (Galatians 6:2)

Encourage one another daily. (Hebrews 3:13)

Confess your sins to one another. (James 5:16)

Pray for one another. (James 5:16)

Submit to one another. (Ephesians 5:21)

Be devoted to one another in brotherly love. (Romans 12:10)

Look at that not even close to complete list. Now ask yourself a question: **Which one of those commands can you obey alone?**

Can you "love one another" in a vacuum? Can you "bear one another's burdens" if you don't know anyone else's burdens and they don't know yours? Can you "forgive one another" if you are never close enough to anyone to get hurt?

You cannot.

If you try to live the Christian life in isolation, you are functionally ignoring over half of the New Testament. You are trying to play the game while sitting on the bench.

The very structure of Jesus' commands requires a community to practice them in. The Church isn't just a place you go to hear a sermon; it is the gymnasium where you work out your salvation. It is the laboratory where you practice the experiments of love, forgiveness, and patience.

Is it messy? Absolutely. People are difficult. They will annoy you, disappoint you, and hurt you. But that isn't a sign that something is wrong with the system; it is the whole point of the system. You can't learn forgiveness without being hurt. You can't learn patience without being annoyed. You can't learn to love fully without "unlovely" people.

The friction of community is the sandpaper God uses to smooth out our rough edges and shape us into the image of His Son.

The Mirror

There is another vital function of community that we miss when we fly solo: **Correction.**

We have talked about sin as *Khata*, missing the mark. The problem with being an archer is that it is very difficult to see your own form while you are shooting. We all have blind spots. We all have patterns of dysfunction that are obvious to everyone around us, but completely invisible to us.

You might think you are just being "assertive", while everyone else sees you as arrogant and abrasive.

You might think you are being "frugal", while everyone else sees you as stingy and greedy.

You might think you are just "venting", while everyone else hears poisonous gossip.

We are masters of self-deception. We rationalize our own dysfunction. We grade ourselves on a curve.

Community acts as a helper.

You need an outside perspective to show you reality. You cannot see your own spiritual blind spots without trusted brothers and sisters who love you enough to tell you the truth.

We need people who are close enough to see our *Khata*, and safe enough to point it out without condemnation. We need people to say, *"Hey, I love you, but I think your aim is off here. You're hurting yourself and the people around you."*

Without that helper, we will continue to miss the mark, convinced the whole time that we are hitting the bullseye.

The First "Not Good"

This truth about our need for connection goes all the way back to the beginning.

In Genesis 1, God creates the universe. After each act of creation, He steps back and declares it *Tov*, Good. Functional. The light is *Tov*. The land is *Tov*. The animals are *Tov*.

Then, in Genesis 2, God creates the first human. He places Adam in a perfect garden. There is no sin, no death, no shame. It is paradise.

And yet, God looks at this man, this perfect being in a perfect world, and for the very first time, He declares something **"Not Good"** (*Lo Tov*).

"The Lord God said, 'It is not good for the man to be alone...'" (Genesis 2:18)

Think about the weight of that statement. Before sin ever entered the world, isolation was already declared dysfunctional.

Why?

Many people assume it was just about biological procreation, Adam needed a partner to make babies. But it goes far deeper than that.

We are created in the *imago Dei*, the Image of God. And the God of the Bible is not a solitary monad. He is a Trinity, Father, Son, and Holy Spirit. God *is* a community of perfect love existing in eternal relationship.

Therefore, if we are made in His image, we are designed for community. We are wired for connection at the deepest level of our being.

To be alone is to be sub-human. It is a violation of our core design specifications. A solitary human is a dysfunctional human.

We were created from connection, for connection. We need others to reflect God's image fully. We need others to practice God's commands functionally. We need others to see ourselves truthfully.

So, if you are tired of the exhausting, lonely trek of the "solo Christian", I invite you to re-read your owner's manual. You were not designed to function alone. The hand needs the body. The Christian needs the Church. It's time to get reconnected. There are always people willing to help. They will be imperfect, but willing. I'm an introvert who is drained in social situations, but the people in my home group are so precious to me.

Don't live life alone.

Chapter 9

The Family Business

Imagine it's Monday morning. The alarm goes off, and you feel that familiar dread settle in your stomach. The weekend is over, and it's time to go back to the "real world", the world of emails, meetings, spreadsheets, diapers, and difficult customers.

Now, contrast that with how you might feel on a Sunday morning, heading to church. You might feel a sense of peace, purpose, and spiritual connection. You feel like you are doing something "holy".

This split between our "sacred" religious life on Sunday and our "secular" work life on Monday is a defining characteristic of the modern Western world. We have drawn a sharp line down the middle of reality.

On one side, we have "Church Work", preaching, worship leading, missionary work. We might think that this is what really matters to God. On the other side, we have "Secular Work", being an accountant, a mechanic, a teacher, a stay-at-home parent. This is just what you do to pay the bills or support your family until you can get back to doing the "real spiritual stuff".

This sacred/secular divide is one of the most dysfunctional and damaging ideas in modern Christianity. It makes most of our waking hours feel spiritually meaningless. It creates a hierarchy where pastors and missionaries are the "professional Christians", and everyone else is just the supporting cast.

But if we put on our Hebrew functional glasses, this entire divide evaporates. In the worldview of the Bible, **there is no such thing as secular work.**

The Prayer and the Plow

To understand this, we need to learn another Hebrew word: **Avodah.**

If you look it up in a dictionary, you will find a surprising definition. *Avodah* means two things simultaneously:

Work/Service (like tilling a field or building a house)

Worship/Ministry (like a priest serving in the temple)

Think about that for a moment. In our language, "work" and "worship" may be opposites. One is what you do for a boss; the other is what you do for God.

But in God's language, they are the exact same word.

To the ancient Hebrew mind, there was no functional difference between a priest offering incense in the Temple and a farmer plowing his field. Both were acts of *Avodah*. Both were service. Both were acts of worship to the Creator.

This is a radical paradigm shift. It means that God doesn't just care about what you do on Sunday morning. He is just as invested in what you do on Monday at 9:00 AM.

When a carpenter builds a table that is sturdy and beautiful (*Tov*), that is *Avodah*. It is an act of worship.

When a programmer writes clean, efficient code that solves a problem, that is *Avodah*.

When a parent changes a dirty diaper with patience and care, that is *Avodah*.

Your prayer and your plow are part of the same idea. They are both ways you serve the Architect of reality.

The First Job Description

To understand our true calling, we have to go back to the Garden. Before there was sin, before there were pastors or churches, there was work.

"The Lord God took the man and put him in the Garden of Eden to work it and keep it." (Genesis 2:15)

God Himself is a Worker. He is a Gardener, a Builder, an Artist. And when He created humans in His image, He made us workers, too. He didn't create Adam and Eve to sit around on clouds playing harps. He created them with a job to do.

They were the **Royal Gardeners**. They were God's representatives on earth, tasked with taking the raw potential of creation and cultivating it.

And what was their core task? We find it in Genesis 1:28: *"fill the earth and **subdue** it."*

Now, the word 'subdue' can sound harsh to our modern ears. It sounds like domination or violent conquest. But in the functional context of Genesis, it means something beautiful.

The world outside the Garden was untamed. It was a place of raw potential, but also a place of chaos.

Our job is to Subdue Dysfunction.

'To subdue' means to bring Function (*Tov*) out of Dysfunction (*Ra*). It means to take chaos and bring it into order. It means to take something broken and make it whole.

This is the fundamental human vocation. We are called to push back against the entropy of the world and create pockets of human flourishing.

When a teacher takes a room full of chaotic, uneducated minds and patiently brings them into the order of knowledge and understanding, they are subduing dysfunction. They are doing the work of Eden.

When an accountant takes a messy pile of receipts and financial chaos and turns it into an organized, functional budget, they are subduing dysfunction.

When a city planner designs a park that turns a vacant, dangerous lot into a safe, beautiful space for community, they are subduing dysfunction.

When a counselor sits with a person whose mind and emotions are in chaos and helps them find a path to healing and wholeness, they are subduing dysfunction.

Do you see? This isn't "secular" work. This is the work of God. It is the work of bringing His Kingdom, His functional order, to bear on a broken world.

The Family Business

When humanity rebelled in the Garden, we were fired from our job as Royal Gardeners. We lost our ability to functionally subdue the earth. Instead of bringing order, we started creating more chaos. Our work became toil, pushing against thorns and thistles.

But the Gospel (Good News) is the story of how Jesus came to restore what was lost. He didn't just come to save our souls for heaven; He came to restore our vocation on earth.

When you become a Christian, you get your badge back as a Royal Gardener.

Jesus looks at you and says, *"You're hired back. I'm restoring you to your original purpose. I'm giving you my Spirit, my Power Source, so you can once again do the work you were created to do."*

This is **The Family Business**. Your Father is the Great Gardener, and He has invited you to join Him in His work.

Your job is to create **'Pockets of Eden'** wherever you go.

You are planted in a specific place, a specific office, neighborhood, family, and city. That is your section of the garden to tend. Your mission is to look around that place and ask: *"Where is the Dysfunction (Ra) here? Where is the chaos? Where is the brokenness?"*

And then, using the gifts, skills, and opportunities God has given you, your job is to bring Function (*Tov*) to that place.

If your workplace is toxic and full of gossip, your job is to be a Pocket of Eden by bringing encouragement, truth, and peace.

If your neighborhood is isolated and lonely, your job is to be a Pocket of Eden by practicing hospitality and building connection.

If your industry is corrupt or exploitative, your job is to be a Pocket of Eden by doing business with integrity and justice.

This is a massive shift for many Christians who are waiting for a "ministry calling". They are waiting for a burning bush or a voice from heaven to tell them to go to seminary or the mission field.

But if you understand the functional worldview, you realize: **You don't need to wait for a calling. You already have one.**

It was given to humanity in Genesis 1. It was restored to you when you started following Jesus.

Your calling is right under your feet. It's in the emails waiting in your inbox. It's in the crying toddler needing your attention. It's in the difficult client you have to deal with.

So, stop waiting for permission to do ministry. Stop dividing your life into "sacred" and "secular" boxes. It's all *Avodah*. It's all worship.

Look at your world. Find the chaos. Roll up your sleeves. And cultivate Eden.

Chapter 10

The Long Defeat

We have spent this entire book talking about how to build a functional life, a life that is aligned with the Architect's design, powered by His Spirit, and dedicated to creating pockets of Eden in a broken world. We have talked about replacing anxiety with purpose, and legalism with love.

It sounds like a recipe for the perfect life, doesn't it? It sounds like if you just get the formula right, if you put in the right fuel, follow the manual, and stay connected to the team, then your machine will run perfectly forever.

I want to tell you that is true. I want to tell you that if you live this way, your marriage will always be happy, your children will never rebel, your business will always prosper, and you will never get sick.

But I would be lying to you. And the Bible never lies to us about the reality of life in a fallen world.

You can build a house perfectly on the rock, but hailstorms still happen.

You can be the best farmer in the world, sowing good seed in good soil, but a drought can still wipe out your harvest. You can be a functional, loving, faithful follower of Jesus, and your life can still fall apart.

The Groaning World

We have to remember where we live. We live in a world that has been fractured by millennia of dysfunction (*Ra*).

The Apostle Paul describes the current state of our universe in Romans 8. He says that creation itself was "subjected to frustration" and is currently "groaning as in the pains of childbirth" (Romans 8:20-22).

Think about that image. The world is groaning. It is in pain. The systems of nature, society, and human bodies are all corrupted by the virus of sin and death.

This means that no matter how functional you are personally, you are still living in a dysfunctional environment. You are trying to build a pristine sandcastle on a beach where the tide is constantly coming in.

The great author J.R.R. Tolkien, who wrote *The Lord of the Rings*, understood this deeply. He was a man who lived through the horrors of two World Wars. He saw the best of human civilization crumble into violence and death.

Tolkien had a phrase for human history outside of paradise. He called it **"The Long Defeat."**

This is a hard concept for us modern Westerners to accept. We are obsessed with progress. We believe that with enough technology, education, and effort, we can solve every problem and create a utopia on earth. We want to win.

But Tolkien, and the Bible, argues that in this life, we are not marching toward inevitable victory. We are fighting a holding action against entropy. We are trying to preserve light in a world that now naturally tends toward darkness. We are trying to build order in a world that naturally inclines toward chaos.

If you measure your life by the world's definition of "winning", constant upward mobility, accumulation of wealth, the eradication of all suffering, you will eventually despair. Because in the end, death "wins". Entropy "wins". The sandcastle gets washed away. But there is still good news.

Re-defining Success: Faithfulness Over Victory

If we are living in "The Long Defeat", how do we keep from giving up? How do we find hope when we know that our best efforts might still end in failure?

We have to redefine success.

In the functional Kingdom of God, success is not measured by "winning". **Success is measured by Faithfulness.**

God does not call us to be successful; He calls us to be faithful. He doesn't ask us to fix the whole world; He asks us to tend the small patch of garden He has entrusted to us.

The prophet Jeremiah preached for decades, and almost no one listened to him. His nation was destroyed. By the world's standards, he was a massive failure. By God's standard, he was a roaring success because he faithfully spoke the word of the Lord.

A mother who faithfully loves and teaches her child, even if that child grows up to reject her faith, is a success in the Kingdom of God. She did her *Avodah*. She was faithful to her calling.

Faithfulness means showing up. It means doing the work of *Tov* (goodness/function) even when it seems futile. It means continuing to build with the grain of the universe even when the whole world seems to be going against it.

This requires a radical shift in our time horizon. We have to stop living for the immediate return on investment. We must become people who are willing to plant trees we will never sit in the shade of or eat from.

We are laying bricks for a building that we will never see finished in our lifetime. We are pouring our lives into people and projects that may not bear fruit for generations.

This feels incredibly inefficient to our modern sensibilities. Judas would probably hate it. But this is the nature of Kingdom work. We are playing the long game.

Nothing Is Wasted

So, if we are fighting a long defeat, and we might never see the fruit of our labor, why bother? Why not just give up and "eat, drink, and be merry, for tomorrow we die"?

Because of the Resurrection.

The resurrection of Jesus is the game-changer. It is the guarantee that "The Long Defeat" is not the final chapter of history. It proves that the Architect has not abandoned His project, and that He has the power to reverse death itself.

Because Jesus rose from the dead, we have a staggering promise, given to us by the Apostle Paul at the end of his massive chapter on the resurrection:

*"Therefore, my dear brothers and sisters, stand firm. Let nothing move you. Always give yourselves fully to the work of the Lord, because you know that **your labor in the Lord is not in vain**."* (1 Corinthians 15:58)

This is the anchor of our hope. "Not in vain." Nothing is wasted.

In a purely materialist universe, everything you do eventually decays into dust. Every act of kindness, every beautiful creation, every moment of love is ultimately swallowed by the heat death of the universe. It's all in vain. It's all hevel (trying to catch vapor).

But in the functional universe of the Bible, the Architect is a master recycler. He does not let any act of *Tov* go to waste.

Every time you choose kindness over anger, you are forging a brick for the New Jerusalem. Every time you do an honest day's work with integrity, you are weaving a thread into the tapestry of the New Creation. Every time you create a pocket of Eden in this broken world, you are creating a prototype of the world to come.

We don't know exactly how it works. But Scripture hints that the "glory and honor of the nations" will be brought into the eternal City of God (Revelation 21:26). The good work we do here, the culture we create, the art we make, the love we share, will somehow survive the fire and be incorporated into the final design.

You are not just shuffling deckchairs on the Titanic. You are building materials for the new ship that is coming.

Your Identity

So, where does this leave us? It leaves us with a new identity and a new mission.

You are not a desperate defendant in a cosmic courtroom trying to prove your innocence. You are a beloved apprentice in the Master's workshop.

Your Identity: A Royal Gardener, restored to your original calling.

Your Enemy: Chaos (*Ra*), dysfunction, and entropy in all its forms.

Your Weapon: Creative Order (*Tov*). Acts of love, beauty, justice, and truth.

Your Power: The Breath of God (*Ruach*), the Holy Spirit who animates your efforts.

Your Hope: The Resurrection, the promise that your work is not in vain.

The world is still groaning. The hailstorms are still coming. You will get tired. You will miss the mark. But you have the manual. You have the power source. And you know the end of the story.

So, get up. Hoist your sail. Head out into the chaos.

And go make something Good.

Chapter 11
The Functional Gospel

If you have made it this far, you know that the language we use matters. We have spent ten chapters stripping away the legal, courtroom language that often makes Christianity sound like a cosmic plea bargain. We have replaced it with the language of the workshop, the garden, and the human body.

Now, it is time to put it all together. It is time to tell the whole story. The story of humanity, of God, and of you, through this new, functional lens.

If you handed this book to a skeptical friend who is allergic to "religious" language, someone who tunes out the moment they hear words like sin, salvation, or repentance, this is how you could tell them the Good News. This is the functional Gospel.

It is a story in six acts, traveling through the timeline of human history, from the dawn of time to the future that is coming.

Act 1: The Design (Creation)

Every great story begins with a setting. Ours begins before time, in the mind of the Great Architect.

God is not a cosmic killjoy waiting to create rules. He is a Master Craftsman, an Artist, and an Engineer of infinite creativity. In the beginning, He designed reality. He built a universe that was complex, beautiful, and perfectly interconnected. It was a finely tuned ecosystem designed for one purpose: human flourishing.

Think of it as a magnificent Garden Machine. Every part had a purpose. The stars provided navigation and seasons. The plants provided food and beauty. The animals provided companionship and labor.

And in the center of it all, He placed His masterpiece: Humanity. We were designed to be the operators of this garden, the Royal Gardeners commissioned to keep it running smoothly and to expand its borders.

When the Architect finished His work, He turned the system on. He watched the stars spin, the plants grow, and the humans interact in perfect harmony. He looked at the entire functional system and declared it *Tov me'od*, very good. Fully operational. It worked perfectly.

There was no friction. No anxiety. No shame. Only flow.

Act 2: The Glitch (The Fall)

But a machine as complex as a human being requires freedom to function truly. A robot can be programmed to obey, but only a free being can choose to love. The Architect wanted partners, not puppets.

So, He gave humanity a choice. He gave them the Owner's Manual, the laws of reality, which was simple: *Stay connected to Me, your Power Source, and you will live. Disconnect from Me to run on your own power, and you will malfunction and die.*

It wasn't a threat; it was a statement of functional reality. Like telling someone, "If you unplug the fan, the blades will stop turning."

The humans designed to run the garden decided they didn't need the Architect's manual. They wanted to be autonomous. They wanted to be the ones to define what was functional and dysfunctional. They chose the DIY approach to reality.

They unplugged themselves from the Source of Life.

This single act introduced a catastrophic virus into the system. The Hebrew Bible calls this virus *Ra*, dysfunction, chaos, evil.

It was an immediate systemic failure. The connection between humans and God was broken (spiritual death). The connection between humans and each other was broken (shame and blame). Even the connection between humans and the earth was broken (toil and thorns).

Since that day, every human being is born with a corrupted operating system. We inherit this dysfunction. We instinctively miss the mark (*Khata*). We aim for love and hit selfishness. We aim for peace and hit anxiety. We damage ourselves, hurt the people around us, and pollute the world with the toxic waste of our dysfunction.

The Garden Machine became a rusty, grinding, dangerous place.

Act 3: The Failed Fixes (Human History)

For centuries, humans have recognized that something is terribly wrong with the world and with ourselves. We know we are malfunctioning. And for centuries, we have tried to fix the glitch ourselves.

We have tried two main approaches, and both have failed.

Approach A: Religion (Outside of the framework God provided His people.) Some tried to fix the glitch by creating elaborate lists of rules to curb the chaos. "If we just have enough laws, enough rituals, enough sacrifices," they thought, "we can force ourselves and others to be functional."

But rules cannot fix a corrupted heart. Religion often just turned people into anxious perfectionists or judgmental hypocrites. Even if it could manage the symptoms of the dysfunction, it couldn't cure the virus. It created the Older Brother in the Prodigal Son story. A dutiful, but bitter and disconnected person.

Approach B: Secularism Others decided the problem was the idea of an Architect altogether. "Let's deny God exists," they said. "We will build paradise ourselves through science, technology, politics, and education. We will be the architects."

This approach has given us amazing technological advancements, but it has not fixed the human heart. We are more connected than ever, yet more lonely. We have more wealth, yet more anxiety. We have tried to build utopia and ended up with the exhausted, polarized, medicated world you see on the news every night.

Nothing worked. The machine was still broken. The harder we tried to fix it on our own, the worse the grinding became.

Act 4: The Mechanic Arrives (Incarnation & Atonement)

But the Architect did not abandon His project. He loved His creation too much to let it spin into oblivion.

He knew that the system could not be fixed from the outside. It required an inside job.

So, the Architect entered the machine Himself.

This is who Jesus is: The Architect in human form. Fully God and fully human. He was born into the chaos, subject to the same fragile biology we are. But because He remained perfectly connected to the Father, the Power Source, He lived the only truly functional human life in history.

He was a walking pocket of Eden. Where there was sickness (*dysfunction*), He brought healing (*function*). Where there was social chaos (outcasts and sinners), He brought relational order (inclusion and love). He showed us what a human being running on the correct operating system and power actually looks like.

But showing us the life wasn't enough. The accumulated toxic waste of human history, the millennia of violence, hatred, and rebellion, had to go somewhere. The Law of Conservation of Dysfunction demanded a cleanup.

So, Jesus went to the Cross. On the cross, He acted as a cosmic filter. He voluntarily opened Himself up to the full force of human *Ra*. He let the virus run its course in His own body. He absorbed the hatred of His enemies, the betrayal of His friends, the injustice of the system, and the ultimate dysfunction of death itself.

He didn't pass the pain on. He swallowed it. When He cried out, "It is finished," He was saying, "The cleanup is complete. The filter has absorbed the toxin." He defeated sin and death.

Act 5: The Reboot (Resurrection)

If the story ended there, Jesus would just be a heroic martyr. But He didn't stay dead.

Three days later, the Architect rebooted the system. Jesus rose from the dead, not just as a resuscitated corpse, but as something entirely new. He was the prototype of a New Humanity, Human Version 2.0.

He had a body that was physical but immortal. A life that was immune to death and dysfunction.

The Resurrection proved that the Architect's design is stronger than the world's dysfunction. It proved that *Tov* (Life) gets the final word over *Ra* (Death). It was the first green shoot pushing through the concrete of a fallen world, signaling that a new spring had begun.

Act 6: The Invitation (Salvation & Mission)

This brings us to today. To you.

Jesus is alive, and He is now offering the same functional life He lived to anyone who wants it. The invitation is simple: **Plug back in.**

He offers to reconnect you to His Power Source, the Spirit, the Breath of God. He offers to download His new operating system into your heart.

He doesn't promise to instantly fix all your glitches. You will still struggle. You will still miss the mark sometimes. You still live in a broken world.

But He promises to be your Master Mechanic. He promises to walk with you, recalibrating your life day by day, teaching you how to aim better, how to hoist your sail to catch His Wind, and how to clean up the messes you make.

And He offers you a job. He invites you to rejoin the Family Business.

He says, *"Take My power. Take My manual. And go back out into your corner of the broken world, your family, your office, your neighborhood. Find the chaos, and use My power to push it back. Create pockets of Eden. Bring order out of disorder. Love the unlovable. Serve the vulnerable. Do good work."*

We are called to be His co-workers, expanding the borders of His functional Kingdom until the day He returns to finish the job. When He comes to wipe away every tear, mend every broken thing, and restore the entire project to the perfect *Tov* He intended from the beginning, it will be the end of the long defeat.

That is the story. It's not about a courtroom. It's about a rescue mission. And you are invited to be part of it.

Chapter 12

The Intellectual Anchor

If you have made it to this final chapter, I suspect you are the type of person who isn't satisfied with just feeling good; you want to know *why* something works. You want to see the schematics. You appreciate intellectual rigor and enjoy seeing how theological concepts map onto the broader landscape of human thought.

Welcome to the workshop's engine room.

Up until now, we have used primarily biblical and agricultural metaphors to describe the "Functional Life". But this framework is not just a religious preference. It is a robust theory of human flourishing that aligns surprisingly well with the deepest insights of ancient philosophy and modern psychology.

For the intellectually curious, this chapter is for you. Let's bolt this theology down to the chassis of "secular" wisdom.

1. Philosophy: The Return to Teleology

For the last few centuries, Western philosophy has been dominated by a single, crushing idea, famously articulated by Jean-Paul Sartre: **"Existence precedes Essence."**

This is the core tenet of atheistic Existentialism. It means that you show up on the scene first (existence), and only later do you define who you are and what your purpose is (essence). There is no "human nature", no pre-existing design, no Architect. You are a blank slate, condemned to be free, forced to invent your own meaning in a meaningless universe.

While this sounds liberating, psychologically, it is a recipe for profound anxiety. It places the infinite weight of defining reality on the shoulders of the finite individual. You have to be your own god.

The Functional worldview flips this script. It argues for what ancient philosophers like Aristotle called **Teleology** (from the Greek *telos*, meaning "end," "purpose," or "goal").

The biblical view is that **"Essence precedes Existence."**

Before you were born, there was a design. There was an intention in the mind of the Architect. You are not a random accident waiting to invent yourself; you are a crafted instrument waiting to make beautiful music.

The existentialist asks in panic: *"What am I supposed to be?"*

The functionalist asks with curiosity: *"What was I designed to be?"*

The functional life is not about the terrifying freedom of self-invention; it is about the relief of **self-discovery**. The Torah (the instruction manual) is not a prison; it is the blueprint that reveals your own inherent structure. Finding your *telos*, your God-given function as a Royal Gardener and Image-Bearer, is the only way to escape the crushing burden of modern self-creation.

2. Psychology: Climbing Maslow's Functional Ladder

You are likely familiar with Maslow's **Hierarchy of Needs**. It's one of the most famous theories in psychology, often presented as a pyramid. Maslow argued that humans must satisfy lower-level basic needs before they can attend to higher-level growth needs.

The Functional biblical worldview doesn't just vaguely align with Maslow's pyramid; it provides a sturdy, engineered scaffolding for climbing it. Let's look at the layers through the lens of *Tov* (Function) and *Ra* (Dysfunction).

The Base: Physiological & Safety Needs (Survival)

Maslow: Food, water, shelter, personal security, order, law, stability.

The Functional View: A society overrun by *Ra* (dysfunction), murder, theft, unchecked greed, chaos, cannot meet these basic needs. Life becomes what Thomas Hobbes called "nasty, brutish, and short".

The Bible (God's manual) is essentially a charter for establishing this base layer of safety. Commandments against murder, theft, and adultery are not arbitrary moralisms; they are the necessary civic engineering required to build a stable platform where human life can survive. You cannot reach higher functional states if you are constantly afraid of being killed or robbed.

The Middle: Love/Belonging & Esteem Needs (Connection & Value)

Maslow: Friendship, intimacy, family, sense of connection, respect, status, recognition, freedom.

The Functional View: The Western "solo Christian" myth utterly fails here. You cannot meet these needs alone.

God's design for the **"Body of Christ"** (the Church community) is the functional answer to the need for belonging. It's a non-transactional community where you are valued not for what you produce, but simply because you are a connected member.

Furthermore, the biblical doctrine of the *Imago Dei* (Image of God) provides an unshakeable foundation for **Esteem**. Your value isn't based on your marketability (a precarious foundation); it is intrinsic to your design as God's representative. The calling to be a Royal Gardener doing your work/worship (*Avodah*) gives every human a dignified, necessary vocation, regardless of their paycheck.

The Peak: Self-Actualization (Fulfilling Your Design)

Maslow: The desire to become the most that one can be; realizing personal potential, self-fulfillment, seeking personal growth and peak experiences.

The Functional View: Secular psychology often struggles to define what a "self-actualized" person actually looks like, sometimes devolving into self-obsession.

The Bible offers a concrete definition: A self-actualized human is one who is fully **functional** (*Tov*). It is a person who perfectly reflects the character of the Architect, loving, creative, truthful, and just, in their own unique context. This is completeness which is the concept of shalom.

Jesus is the ultimate example of a self-actualized human. He is the prototype. The goal of the Christian life ("being conformed to the image of Christ") is the pursuit of true self-actualization, becoming the fully human, fully alive person you were designed to be.

3. The Mechanics of Change: CBT and Repentance

How do we actually move from dysfunction to function? Modern psychology offers a powerful tool called **Cognitive Behavioral Therapy (CBT)**. The core idea of CBT is that our thoughts create our feelings and behaviors. If you have distorted thoughts ("I'm worthless," "The world is dangerous"), you will have dysfunctional emotions and actions (anxiety, avoidance).

The goal of CBT is **Cognitive Restructuring**, identifying lies you believe and replacing them with the truth.

This is almost a perfect secular mirror of the biblical concept of **Repentance**.

As we discussed, repentance isn't just feeling sad. The Greek word is *metanoia*, which literally means a "change of mind". It is the act of realizing, *"Wait, the way I'm thinking about this is wrong (dysfunctional). I need to align my thinking with reality (God's truth)."*

The Dysfunction (*Ra*): You believe the lie that your worth equals your productivity. This leads to anxiety and burnout.

The CBT/Repentance Fix: You identify the lie. You look at the Owner's Manual (Scripture) which says your worth is intrinsic as God's image-bearer. You actively practice replacing the lie with the truth. You recalibrate your aim.

The Functional lens provides the ultimate framework for CBT because it provides an objective standard of Truth, the Architect's design, against which we can test our distorted thoughts.

Data Supports Design

Finally, it is worth noting that modern research continues to uncover data that supports the functional design outlined in Scripture.

The Sabbath Effect: Numerous studies have shown that regular periods of rest and "detachment from work" are crucial for preventing burnout, increasing creativity, and maintaining mental health. The ancient command to rest one day in seven is not a religious hoop to jump through; it's biological wisdom.

The Altruism Paradox: Psychologists have repeatedly found that people who are generous with their time and money (volunteering, donating) have lower rates of depression and higher levels of happiness than those who focus on acquiring wealth for themselves. Jesus' functional teaching that "it is more blessed to give than to receive" (Acts 20:35) is empirically verifiable.

The Power of Forgiveness: Holding onto grudges (the Cycle of Vengeance) has been linked to higher blood pressure, heart rate, and levels of stress hormones. Forgiveness, the act of absorbing the cost and letting go, is now widely recognized in therapeutic settings as essential for emotional and even physical health.

A Unified Theory

The "Functional Life" is not a retreat from reason into blind faith. It is a move toward a more unified, integrated view of reality.

It is a worldview where the deepest intuitions of philosophy, the structural necessities of psychology, and the revealed truths of Scripture all converge. It is a theory that doesn't just make sense in a seminary classroom; it makes sense in a therapist's office, in a physics lab, and in the daily grind of being a human.

God is the author of all truth. We shouldn't be surprised when the book of nature and the book of Scripture tell the same story. The Architect knows what He is doing.

Afterword

The Mainspring and the Vapor

You have reached the end of the book. You've walked through the workshop, looked at the blueprints, and hopefully, traded your legal glasses for functional ones or at least added a new viewpoint. We have covered a lot of ground, from the Garden of Eden to philosophy, from ancient Hebrew word studies to modern psychological theories.

It can feel like a lot to take in. When you are faced with a paradigm shift this size, the most common reaction is paralysis. You might be thinking, *"Okay, I get it. My old way of living was dysfunctional. This new way sounds better. But where do I even start? Do I need to quit my job? Sell my possessions? Learn Hebrew?"*

Please, don't do any of those things unless it is functional for you and probably not right away.

The beauty of the functional life is that it doesn't require a massive, dramatic overhaul of your external circumstances. It starts with a quiet, internal realignment.

The Lesson of the Smoke

Before we get to the practical steps, I want to leave you with one final image from the Bible's ultimate book on functionality: Ecclesiastes.

The author of Ecclesiastes, The Teacher, spent his entire life running a massive experiment. He had nearly unlimited wealth, power, and wisdom. He decided to try everything the world had to offer to see what actually worked, what was actually *Tov*.

He built massive projects. He amassed gold and silver. He pursued pleasure, knowledge, and fame. He tried it all.

And his conclusion?

"Hevel, hevel. Everything is hevel."

This is often translated as "Meaningless! Meaningless!" which makes him sound like a depressed philosopher. But the Hebrew word *Hevel* literally means "**vapor**" or "**smoke**".

He isn't saying that life is morally bad. He is saying it is functionally elusive.

Imagine trying to grab a handful of smoke. You can see it. It looks solid. But the moment you close your hand around it, it slips through your fingers. You can't hold onto it.

The Teacher realized that trying to find ultimate satisfaction, security, or purpose in the temporary things of this world like money, career, status, or even pleasure, is like trying to grab smoke. It is dysfunctional. It doesn't work. It leaves you empty-handed and brokenhearted.

You were designed for something solid. You were made by an eternal Architect, and your soul will never find rest in vapor.

The Mainspring

So, if everything is vapor, what is left? How do we build a life that doesn't just slip through our fingers?

The Teacher concludes his book with the answer: **"Fear God and keep his commandments, for this is the whole duty of man."** (Ecclesiastes 12:13)

This isn't a return to legalism. It's the ultimate functional conclusion. He is saying: *"The only way to navigate through the smoke without crashing is to stay connected to the Architect. The only thing solid is Him."*

Think about an old-fashioned mechanical watch. It has dozens of tiny gears, springs, and cogs, all designed to work together in perfect harmony. When they do, the watch tells the time accurately. It is *Tov.*

But all of those gears are powered by one central component: the mainspring. If the mainspring isn't wound, nothing else moves.

You can polish the glass face of the watch all day. You can adjust the tiny hands. You can admire the complexity of the gears. But if you don't wind the mainspring, the watch is functionally dead.

For too long, many of us have been obsessively polishing the outside of our lives, trying to look good, trying to follow the rules, trying to manage our behavior. We have been fiddling with the gears of our finances, our schedules, and our relationships, trying to force them to work without power. We've been chasing smoke.

It's time to wind the mainspring.

Jesus knew this. The religious leaders of His day were masters of gear-management. They had 613 individual commandments, tiny cogs they polished obsessively. One day, a lawyer asked Jesus, "Teacher, which is the greatest commandment in the Law?" He was essentially asking, "Which gear is the most important?"

Jesus didn't point to a gear. He pointed to the mainspring.

"Jesus replied: 'Love the Lord your God with all your heart and with all your soul and with all your mind.' This is the first and greatest commandment. And the second is like it: 'Love your neighbor as yourself.' All the Law and the Prophets hang on these two commandments." (Matthew 22:37-40)

When Jesus says everything hangs on these two commands, He is giving us a functional reality. He is saying: *"If you get these two things right, the whole machine works. If you get them wrong, nothing else matters."*

Loving God is plugging into the Power Source, the only solid thing in a world of vapor. Loving your neighbor is the resulting flow of current.

Everything we have talked about in this book, finding your calling as a Royal Gardener, learning to rest, practicing forgiveness, becoming a pocket of Eden, all of it is just the natural outflow of a life centered on loving God and loving people.

Three Small Steps to Wind the Spring

So, how do you apply this? Don't try to fix your whole life by tomorrow. Start by winding the mainspring. Here are three very small, very practical steps you can take starting today.

1. The 10-Minute Hoist (Connection before Action) Before your feet hit the floor in the morning, before you check your phone, before the chaos of the day begins, take ten minutes. Do not try to be productive. Don't even open your Bible to study it, although that is a great morning addition. Just sit.

Acknowledge that you are a sailboat and that you have no power of your own. Say something simple like: *"Father, everything else is vapor. You are the rock. I am unplugged. I cannot love well today on my own battery. I am hoisting my sail. Fill me with your Breath (Ruach)."*

Then, sit in silence. Just be with the Architect. This simple act of daily recalibration is one of the most functional things you can do to start your day.

2. The "Pocket of Eden" Audit (Seeing the Chaos) Sometime today, look at your immediate environment, your office cubicle, your kitchen, your email inbox. Identify one small area of chaos (*Ra*). Maybe it's a literal mess, or maybe it's a strained relationship with a coworker.

Don't try to fix the whole world. Just pick that one small area and ask the Holy Spirit: *"How can I bring a little bit of good(Tov) to this specific chaos today?"*

It might mean organizing a drawer. It might mean sending an encouraging text to that difficult coworker. It might mean simply doing your next task with excellence and integrity. Do that one thing as an act of worship (*Avodah*).

3. The Mirror Check (Breaking Isolation) Find one other person, a spouse, a friend, a mentor, and tell them you read this book. Tell them one thing that resonated with you.

Then, ask them a brave question: *"I'm learning about 'missing the mark.' Do you see any blind spots in my life? Is there a way I am acting dysfunctionally that I can't see?"*

Give them permission to be a mirror. And then, this is the hard part, just listen. Don't defend yourself. Just say "Thank you". Then, take it to the Architect in prayer.

A Final Thank You

Thank you for taking the time to read this book. I know that adding a point of view can be uncomfortable work. It can feel disorienting to take off the glasses you've worn your whole life.

But I believe the discomfort is worth it.

You were not created to live a life of anxious, exhausting rule-keeping. You were not created to chase smoke and end up empty-handed.

You were designed for something far more beautiful, exciting, and life-giving. You were designed to be a partner with God in the restoration of all things.

The Workshop is open. The Master Craftsman is waiting. You have the manual, and you have access to the power.

Go live functionally and enjoy the life that God gave you.

Trust Him, love Him, and love the people you interact with.

This is good.